The Amazing Life of Rita Rizzo

The Early Years of Mother Mary Angelica

D1615793

Barbara A. Gaskell

Illustrated by Peggy A. Dolensky

St. Raphael Center, Inc

Canton, Ohio

All scripture quotes were taken from the King James Bible

St. Raphael Center, Inc
4365 Fulton Drive N.W.
Canton, Ohio 44718
www.CatholicBook.net

Illustrated by **Peggy A. Dolensky**

The Amazing Life of Rita Rizzo/ Barbara A. Gaskell – 1st ed.
ISBN 978-1-7336090-1-2

This book is dedicated to "Team Angelica," a faithful group of volunteers who have selflessly given of their time and talent to establish the **Mother Angelica Tour.** Pilgrims who will come from around the world to visit the hometown of Mother Angelica will be forever indebted to you. I thank you for your hard work and love of the Catholic Faith. May God bless you abundantly.

www.MotherAngelicaTour.com

Contents

The Backdrop 9

The Catholic Faith 15

The Church...19

Suffering...27

High School...31

The Illness..33

Rhoda Wise..37

The Healing...43

The Call..47

Trial Period...53

Sancta Clara Monastery...57

Renovations...61

The Injury...69

Our Lady of the Angels Monastery....................................75

History of Accomplishments..81

Discussion Questions...87

Introduction

In 1981, Mother Angelica, a cloistered Franciscan nun, launched what has become the largest religious media network in the world: Eternal Word Television Network. She began this network with $200 in a monastery garage in Birmingham, Alabama. EWTN now reaches 264 million homes in 145 countries and over 700 million homes with AM, FM, shortwave radio and internet.

It all began in 1923, in a small home in the southeast end of Canton, Ohio. Born Rita A. Rizzo, the future Mother Angelica, grew up in a working class neighborhood during the Roaring Twenties a block away from her parish church.

Young Rita had a difficult childhood. Her father John abandoned the family before Rita was five years old. Divorce soon followed. Life was a struggle for Rita and her mother. Rita's years of trial were compounded by a debilitating stomach ailment until she was healed by Jesus through a woman named Rhoda Wise. That healing set her life on a course that would ultimately change the world........   Here is her story.

The Backdrop

Rita Antoinette Rizzo entered the world on April 20, 1923…weighing just shy of 12 pounds. She was born in her parents' bedroom at 824 Court Ave, just two blocks north of the railroad tracks in Canton, Ohio. Her father, John, was a 29-year-old tailor born in Italy and her mother, Mae was a 23-year-old housewife. It was the young couple's first and only child.

Rita's early life was turbulent at best. Her parents had an explosive relationship. Court records show that John Rizzo was an abusive husband. Not only was he verbally and mentally abusive to his wife Mae but he was physically abusive on numerous occasions. A month after the birth of their daughter Rita, John beat his wife severely. John was a womanizer and when Rita was five years old he abandoned his family. He pulled up stakes and went to California for more than a year. During that time he sent his wife and daughter a total of $30, a paltry sum even in 1928.

Because of John's lack of support Mae and Rita were forced to move in with Mae's parents. Anthony and Mary Gianfrancesco were well known in the Italian community. Rita's grandparents helped new Italian immigrants find work. They ran a family friendly tavern attached to their home at 1029 Liberty Ave in the southeast end of Canton. It was a very popular place during Prohibition. Mae's brothers Peter, Nick and Frank also lived in the family home. It made for crowded quarters but the three generations co-existed.

At Rita's birth in 1923, Prohibition was in full swing. The 18th amendment to the U. S. Constitution, also known as "Prohibition" was the nationwide ban on the production, importation, transportation, and sale of alcoholic beverages. The law remained in place from 1920 to 1933. By most accounts, Prohibition wasn't so dry after all. Those years were usually associated with speakeasies, bootleggers, bathtub gin and gangsters. History has since shown that Prohibition led to such unintended consequences as the explosive growth of urban crime organizations. One such organization was the Italian "Black Hand."

The "Black Hand" was a notorious Italian group that terrorized Canton, Ohio in the 1920's. The city was so extremely corrupt with bootlegging, red-light districts, extortion, gambling, and dirty cops, that it was known as "Little Chicago."

The editor of the Canton Daily News, Don Mellett, won a Pulitzer Prize for reporting on the corruption in the city of Canton and shortly thereafter was ambushed and assassinated in his garage at the age of 34. It was 1926. Rita Rizzo was three years old. The Chief of Detectives of the City of Canton and three others were convicted of his murder. They spent the rest of their lives in prison for the crime. It was a brutal murder which made national headlines. The Italian "Black Hand" had taken their revenge.

Rita experienced first-hand the effects of Prohibition and the strangling grip of the Black Hand in her small world. Rita grew up in the Italian neighborhood one block east of South Cherry Avenue. The area was home to saloons, gambling dens and brothels. It was known in the 1920's as "the Jungle."

The New York Times

March 17, 1910

Pope Pius X appointed Rev. J. Adolph Cascianelli, pastor of St. Anthony Italian Roman Catholic Church of Canton, Ohio to fill an appointment to investigate the Italian situation in the United States in an effort to get at the root of Italian crime, particularly "Black Hand" outrages.

The SPREAD of the BLACK HAND

MILLIONAIRE IS DRIVEN TO EXILE BY BLACK HAND

Italian Murder-Methods Now Organizing Throughout the United States.

A Perilous Condition that Must Be Sternly Abolished.

FEAR IN THE BRONX OF THE BLACK HAND

Residents of Washingon Avenue Are Scared by Threatening Letters.

ASK FOR PROTECTION.

NINE DIE BY FIRE

SET BY BLACK HAND.

Blackmail Had Been Refused and Tenement House Was Set Ablaze.

EXPLODE BOMB IN HOUSE WHICH POLICE GUARDED

Black Hand Agents Again Try to Wreck Tenement Owned by Francesco Spinelli.

LIVES OF 10,000 IN PERIL BY BLACK HAND, BINGHAM HELPLESS

BLACK-HAND OUTRAGES CAUSE NEW REIGN OF TERROR

THIS LESSON SPELLED "DEATH"--THOUSANDS IN TERROR SINCE NEW YORK BLACK HAND MASSACRE

Reprinted from www.gangrule.com

The Catholic Faith

The Catholic Faith was obligatory for most Italian families and Rita's family was no different. Young Rita was baptized at St. Anthony Catholic Church on September 19, 1923. The pastor was shocked that the parents waited so long. Rita was six months old. After Father performed the baptism, Rita's mother Mae carried her to a side altar dedicated to Our Lady of Sorrows. She placed the baby on the altar and said, 'I give you my daughter,' Mother Angelica remembered, a bit sadly, "I'm sure she thought she would have other children, but she never did." [1]

Mae's words were prophetic. The future Mother Angelica was to experience an incredible amount of physical and emotional pain and suffering in her life.

_____

The Seven Sorrows of Mary

The Prophecy of Simeon.

The Flight into Egypt.

The Loss of the Child Jesus in the Temple

The Meeting of Mary and Jesus on the Way of the Cross

The Crucifixion of Jesus on Mount Calvary.

The Piercing of the side of Jesus with a spear, and His descent from the Cross.

The Burial of Jesus.

Rita turned five in 1928 and later that year her mother filed for divorce. Mae and her daughter were devastated by John's abandonment of their family.

Adding to their misery, the Stock Market crashed and the Great Depression hit in October of 1929. Bank accounts were wiped out, loans were foreclosed and millions were out of work. Mae was without a husband and father for her daughter. But she was determined to support herself and her daughter so she began to offer her services by washing, ironing and dry cleaning laundry. Her husband John was a tailor so she knew a bit about the care of clothing.

Mae began to spend time volunteering at St. Anthony Catholic Church where her daughter Rita was enrolled in school. She found some solace in her church family but she and Rita had to deal with the constant shame of divorce. Disapproving looks and whispering followed them.

CHAPTER 3

The Church

St. Anthony Catholic Church was just finishing a building project. The pastor, Fr. Joseph Riccardi had been working to relocate St. Anthony Church, It had been an intense battle. The original structure at 918 Liberty Street was just a block north of the GianFrancesco homestead. It was a wooden frame structure built as a mission church for the Italian community. The church was in desperate need of repair. It contained no heating system and general deterioration made it an impossible situation.

Fr. Riccardi pleaded his case to Bishop Schrembs. A generous woman was willing to donate enough land to build a church, school and rectory a half a mile east on 11th Street. But the "Liberty Street" shop owners were adamantly opposed to the move. They wanted the new church built on the present site. The parish church was the only respectable feature in an area of pool halls, beer joints and brothels. Men loitered around the church making iliicit deals but very seldom attending services.

Bishop Schrembs tried to mediate the situation. The Bishop gave the "Liberty Street" gang the opportunity to prove their case; garner enough pledges to rebuild the parish church on the current site within four months and he would concede. When the deadline arrived less than half of the required amount was pledged. The die was cast. But the Liberty Street group would not yield so easily. They grew more agitated and instigated dissent. The group filed a lawsuit trying to thwart the move that Fr. Riccardi favored.

Plans moved forward for the diocese to accept the generous donation of two acres of property on 11th Street. The lot was large enough for a church, school and parish house. Fr. Riccardi requested restrictions upon the properties around the new church site "against pool-rooms, dives, and other undesirable places of amusement." [2] He was concerned for his flock especially the children and young people of his parish. Fr. Riccardi wanted a respectable neighborhood for Italian parents to raise their families.

But all was not well. The shop owners near the old church site who made their livelihood by the moral corruption of the Italian young people were infuriated. Their cloak of respectability was gone.

One Sunday morning after the new church was dedicated, Fr. Riccardi had offered the 9:30am Mass. A young woman and her 5 year old daughter sat in the last pew during the service. After

Mass Father went to the back vestibule of the church to prepare for a baptism. As he approached the last pew he recognized the young woman and greeted her and her daughter. The woman followed after him. When they reached the vestibule she pulled a revolver from under her coat and shot him point blank. He died several hours later.

After the shooting the young woman went outside to wait for the police to arrive and arrest her, holding bystanders at bay with her gun. When police arrived she surrendered the revolver. They arrested her and took her into custody. Her husband was arrested shortly after the shooting. He was questioned and released several hours later.

The shooting was a national sensation. Every major newspaper across the country reported the brutal murder. The murder trial lasted ten days. The courtroom overflowed its capacity. The jury acquitted her by reason of "temporary insanity." Several days after the trial she was examined again and found "sane" by the courts and was set free. Rita Rizzo was six years old.

Bishop Schrembs of Cleveland spoke with Fr. Riccardi as he lay dying. The Bishop told the local newspaper he believed that the young woman may have been "used as an instrument of vengeance."

"Fr Riccardi was fighting for the building of a decent, clean-living Italian colony in Canton, free from the influence of gambling places, bootlegging joints and infamous houses which infested the neighborhood of the old location." Bishop Schrembs said. "He sacrificed his life for the clean, wholesome lives of the Italians of Canton."[3]

Today a building on the St. Anthony Church campus bears his name.

"It was terrible. The murder rocked our parish to its foundation. No one was ever punished for the crime." Mother Angelica said on *Mother Angelica Live*

CHAPTER 4

The Suffering

Two years to the day of the shooting of Fr. Riccardi the Rizzo divorce decree was made final. The court awarded final custody of young Rita, now 8, to her mother, Mae. Her father, John, was instructed to pay five dollars a week as child support. The support never came. That's when "Hell began for us." Said Mother Angelica, "I used to wonder if there was nothing in this world for us but suffering." [4] For years Rita didn't understand the cruelty of her classmates and teachers who belittled her because she came from a broken marriage. She gradually became completely isolated. Her main concern was taking care of her mother who suffered from severe bouts of depression.[5]

"I did very poorly in school," Mother Angelica remembered later. "I wasn't interested in the capital of Ohio. I was interested in whether my mother had committed suicide that day." [6]

Rita attended St. Anthony School until the fifth grade. The teaching nuns who should have encouraged her instead demeaned her. After one especially cruel occurrence, her mother marched down to the rectory and pulled Rita out of school. "I hated those nuns, hated them." Mother Angelica remembered.[7]

Mae and Rita moved out of the GianFrancesco homestead and lived in a series of one room apartments for the next several years. "Sometimes I wondered if there was a God, and if there was such a person I couldn't figure out why He wouldn't let me have a family like the other kids." [7]

During those years Mae became heavily dependent upon her daughter as Mae suffered from severe bouts of depression. Young Rita became a

provider for them. She delivered the laundry to Mae's customers and did everything she could to help her Mother make a living. Without any support from her father, life was terribly difficult for the two of them. By the time Rita was a freshman at McKinley High School, her mother, was close to a nervous breakdown and finances forced them to return to the GianFrancesco homestead.

CHAPTER 5

High School

Rita began high school in 1937 at the age of fourteen. Her classmates remembered her as a loner. One of the McKinley High School teachers invited Rita to become a drum majorette so she took up baton twirling. She became so proficient at it that she ultimately gave lessons at Gattuso Music in downtown Canton. Rita's earnings provided income for her and her mother.

Rita's nerves were frayed. She tried to balance her studies, her work and caring for her mother. Mae suffered a nervous breakdown and went to spend time with her sister Rose in Philadelphia. Rita's grades suffered. By her junior year she had flunked several classes and needed to complete summer school. Rita's majorette days were over. Rita felt that things couldn't get much worse. She was wrong.

CHAPTER 6

The Illness

During her junior year at McKinley High School Rita began to suffer stomach spasms. Rita concealed the problem from her mother. She tried to ignore the spasms but the pain would not go away. Sometimes the pain was so severe that Rita doubled over in agony. But Rita forged ahead going to school, delivering the dry cleaning for her mother and trying to live a somewhat normal life. The situation gradually deteriorated. Every time Rita ate food it felt as if there were shards of glass tearing through her stomach. By her senior year in high school Rita had lost twenty pounds. The family doctor was called in. He diagnosed Rita with a "dropped stomach" or a condition called "ptosis" of the stomach.

A special medical belt was designed for Rita which made the situation tolerable. She graduated from high school that year and landed a job at

The Timken Roller Bearing Company. Just six months after graduation Japan attacked Pearl Harbor and the United States was thrust into World War II. The Timken Company hummed with activity and young Rita began to exhibit her natural leadership skills. She worked in the advertising department. Her supervisor, Peter Poss, thought highly of her. "Rita impressed her boss, he thought she was great," said Elsie Machuga, her high school friend. [9]

But Rita's stomach spasms continued to worsen, sometimes driving her to the lady's lounge at work where she could find relief only by lying down. Her stomach was so twisted she could only eat crackers and tea. Solid food was not an option. The doctor prescribed a surgical corset and encouraged her to sleep with her feet raised above her head. At one point Rita found that her abdomen had turned a bluish color and a large lump appeared.

Rita's downward spiral continued and Mae Rizzo was desperate to help her daughter. One January afternoon in 1943, Mae Rizzo shared her deep concerns about Rita with an acquaintance, Catherine Barthel, as they rode the bus home. Catherine encouraged Mae to take Rita to see

Rhoda Wise. Catherine related an incredible story of a local woman, Rhoda Wise, who had been miraculously healed by Jesus a few years earlier. Mae contacted Mrs. Wise that very evening. Mrs. Wise graciously accepted the visitors even though the hour was late.

CHAPTER 7

Rhoda Wise

Rhoda Wise lived with her husband, George and daughter, Anna Mae. She had suffered from severe intestinal problems for years. At the age of 44, she had a 39 pound tumor removed from her abdomen. The operation appeared to be a success. The year was 1932. Four years later Rhoda fell and seriously injured her ankle. Her doctor advised that the injury was permanent. She was fitted with crutches and endured a series of leg casts. Chronic pain lingered.

In 1938, Rhoda returned to Mercy Hospital, the local Catholic hospital, to be fitted with a new cast. The nurses discovered that she had developed an abscess at her abdominal incision. Upon further inspection Rhoda was found to have adhesions. During a ten month hospitalization, Rhoda underwent three surgeries resulting in a perforated bowel and leaving her with a hole in her abdomen that would not heal. The contents of the bowel oozed from her wound continually necessitating frequent dressing of the wound daily.

During her long stay in the hospital, Rhoda became interested in the Catholic faith. One of the nursing sisters, Sr. Clement, taught Rhoda how to pray the rosary. Sister Clement also taught her about St. Therese of Liseiux, the Little Flower. These two devotions led Rhoda to convert to Catholicism while she was in the hospital. On January 1, 1939 Rhoda was received into the Catholic Church by Msgr. George Habig, pastor of St. Peter Catholic Church. Two months later, Bishop James McFadden conferred the sacrament of Confirmation on Rhoda in her hospital sickbed.

By May of 1939, the medical community had exhausted all their options and informed Rhoda there was nothing more they could do for her. The doctors finally released her from the hospital with the diagnosis of incurable. She was sent home to die. Rhoda returned to her tiny three room "Depression" shack located next to the city dump in the northeast end of Canton. A visiting nurse came daily to change the dressing on her wound.

The smell was foul and the continuous draining made Rhoda's abdomen raw, inflicting intense pain.

Three weeks later, on May 28th, Rhoda lay in bed in great anguish. It was 2:45am. Suddenly a brilliant light shone in the bedroom. When Rhoda turned to see the source, much to her astonishment, she saw Jesus Christ sitting in a chair beside her bed. He was "robed in a gold garment that reflected every color." * Rhoda thought that He had come to take her to heaven but Our Lord said, " No, your time has not yet come. I will return in thirty-one days." * She reached out to touch him but he disappeared.

Excerpted from "The Rhoda Wise Story" at www.rhodawise.com

In the days that followed, Rhoda, in her agony, prayed for death if she could not be healed. As he promised, Jesus returned on June 28th , again in the wee hours of the morning but this time St. Therese, the Little Flower, was with Him. St. Therese motioned for Rhoda to remove the bandage from her abdomen. The saint put her hand on Rhoda's abdomen and the wound was instantly healed!

There was great rejoicing among Rhoda's family, Msgr. Habig, Sr. Clement, Rhoda's friends and relatives. In the months that followed large numbers of people began to visit Rhoda after this amazing healing.

Meanwhile, Rhoda, even though her abdomen was healed, was still dealing with her leg cast. Two months later, Rhoda was fitted with another cast. On August 15, she sat in her bed crying from the pain of her tight fitting cast. In the middle of the night, her bedroom became brilliantly light and there stood St. Therese. " 'Stand up and walk,' said the saint. I placed my feet on the floor and stood up and as I did, the cast, over a foot long, split open from top to bottom and I easily stepped out of it." * St.Therese then told Rhoda to "Go to church," and disappeared.

Excerpted from "The Rhoda Wise Story" at www.rhodawise.com

"I, who had not walked without crutches for over two and a half years, I found that my foot was again perfectly straight and sound, and I walked quite freely about the house. At 6:00 A.M. I was taken by automobile to Mercy Hospital, where I walked from the elevator to the chapel, a distance of some 60 yards, without the slightest assistance. I then heard Mass for the first time in my life. It was the feast of

the Assumption of the Blessed Virgin Mary. I have been walking without difficulty ever since."

Excerpted from "Her Name Means Rose" by Karen Sigler, OSF

Rhoda was so grateful for the many blessings that God gave her, she offered herself to Our Lord as a "victim soul" – one who suffers for the welfare of others.   Jesus accepted her offer and for several years (1942-1945) until the end of WW II – she suffered from the visible stigmata in her hands and feet and three wounds in her forehead which bled profusely on First Fridays.

Jesus and St. Therese appeared to Rhoda often sometimes alone, sometimes together in the nine years between her cure and her death. But they always came together on June 28th; the anniversary of her first cure. Thousands of pilgrims flocked to Rhoda's home as word spread. There were many conversions and many cures……………one of them was Rita Rizzo, the future Mother Angelica.

CHAPTER 8

The Healing

On January 8, 1943, Rita Rizzo entered Rhoda Wise's home for the first time. She sat in "Our Lord's chair" and Rhoda gave Rita a novena to St. Therese of Lisieux. Rhoda told Rita to pray the novena to obtain a cure for her stomach ailment. Rita did as instructed and nine days later she was completely healed!

This was a turning point for the young Rita Rizzo. Later in life the future Mother Angelica would say, *"When the Lord came in and healed me I had a different attitude. I knew there was a God and that he loved me. I didn't know that before. After I was healed, all I wanted to do was give my life to Jesus."* [10]

"I remember when Rita was healed," said her cousin Joanne. "We lived next to each other. She came out in the back yard jumping around and saying she was healed. 'Punch me in the stomach, Joanne. See I'm healed.' she said to me.[11]

Everything changed for Rita Rizzo from that point forward.

After Rita was healed she wanted to learn all she could about this Savior who had changed her life. She was eager to grow in holiness so she turned for guidance to the holiest person she knew, Rhoda Wise. Rita began to volunteer at the Rhoda Wise Home.

As word spread of the healings and conversions that were taking place at the Rhoda Wise Home, thousands of pilgrims began coming to see her. Volunteers were needed to help with the crowds that came to see Rhoda and answer the hundreds of letters sent to her asking for prayers. Young Rita began to help with answering the letters, sending out Sacred Heart badges and St. Therese prayer cards. Some volunteers helped by cooking meals, others washed the clothes that covered Rhoda's stigmata.

The stigmata is a term used to describe the manifestations of bodily wounds corresponding to the crucifixion wounds of Jesus Christ, such as the hands, feet, side and crown of thorns. Every first Friday, for more than two years, Rhoda bled from these wounds similar to the wounds of Christ. Witnessing this had a profound influence on young Rita Rizzo. She developed a deep devotion to the sufferings of Jesus.

Rita began to take her Catholic Faith seriously. She began reading spiritual books and performing devotional practices. She began to attend Mass as often as possible. Many weekdays, after her work at the Timken Company, she would ride the bus to St. Anthony Catholic Church and pray the Stations of the Cross before going home for supper. Rita recognized her own sorrowful life in the way of the cross she walked with Jesus every afternoon.

CHAPTER 9

The Call

One Autumn afternoon in 1943 Rita stopped at St. Anthony Catholic Church to pray the Stations of the Cross as was her custom. After finishing the Stations, Rita knelt, as usual, before the statue of Our Lady of Sorrows, the same statue that her mother had placed her before on her Baptism day. While kneeling before Our Lady, Rita was overcome with a deep sense that Jesus was calling her to a deeper relationship with Him. "I had the unquestioning knowledge that I was to become a nun."[12]

Rita distinctly heard, with the ear of her heart, Our Lord calling her to give her life to Him as a nun but she was disturbed at the idea. She hated the nuns who had taught her because of their cruelty but here was Jesus asking her to become one! Secondly, Rita knew her mother would never agree to this path for her life. Her mother had become completely dependent upon her and would be unwilling to let Rita go. Yet Rita was resolved to say "yes" to Her Savior. Like the apostles that saw the risen Lord, Rita was at once overjoyed yet terrified.

Msgr. George Habig was the spiritual advisor of Rhoda Wise and the pastor of St. Peter Catholic Church. Young Rita decided if anyone could help her in this situation he could. Several days later, Rita finally divulged her secret to Msgr. Habig; God was calling her to become a nun. He was not surprised. After her healing he had been watching her spiritual transformation for months and he was delighted to hear the news. When Rita explained the difficult situation with her mother, Msgr. Habig agreed that it would be best not to tell her mother of her calling.

With Msgr. Habig's encouragement Rita decided to investigate the Josephite Sisters in Buffalo, New York. Rita avoided telling her mother about her plans by concocting a story that she would be visiting a friend over the weekend. Her mother was suspicious but let her go.

When the truth came out days later, Mae flew into a rage accusing young Rita of abandoning her. Rita resolved to continue the search but to be more cautious.

The Josephite Sisters wrote to Rita informing her that they would consider her as a potential member but felt she was better suited to a contemplative order. Rita consulted Msgr. Habig who encouraged her to visit the St. Paul Shrine in Cleveland, Ohio. The Shrine is home to the Poor Clares of Perpetual Adoration, a Franciscan contemplative order. This time Rita was able to visit the Sisters in Cleveland during a work day, so her mother was none the wiser.

Rita felt that the St. Paul Shrine was a great fit. She couldn't wait to return. The feeling was mutual. The Poor Clare Sisters invited her to enter their order on August 15th. Rita prayed about this momentous decision. On August 15, 1944 Rita left her house for the workday at the Timken Company as usual, but instead of going to work, her supervisor, Peter Poss, drove her to the bus station, paid for her ticket to Cleveland and promised to deliver a handwritten letter to Rita's mother explaining Rita's decision. The letter read in part:

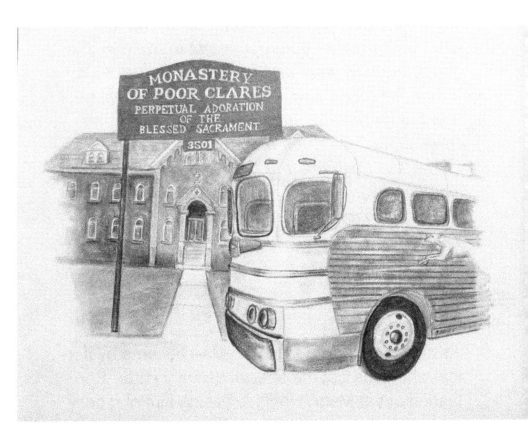

Dear Mother,

I know this is a shock to you but had I asked your permission you would not have granted it.......To enter this way has hurt me tremendously...I wanted you to give me to Our Lord as His Spouse...It may be difficult for you to understand but this is God's Holy Will...........Your work is on the outside winning souls for Him......A cloister, my mother, is heaven on earth......I love you and have not forgotten what you have done for me......Please Trust Our Lord...You can write to me and visit me every two months...I love you very much.

Rita [13]

As anticipated, Rita's mother Mae became hysterical when she got the special delivery letter. She lashed out at Msgr. Habig accusing him of a conspiracy to take her daughter away from her. It was a terrible scene.

CHAPTER 10

The Trial Period

Rita entered the St. Paul Shrine with great joy and abandonment. She was destined to live, pray and work within the confines of her monastery. Her new life was to be a "prisoner of love;" love of the Blessed Sacrament. The Poor Clares of Perpetual Adoration are a cloistered order, dedicated to the adoration of Jesus in the Blessed Sacrament. A cloistered order means that the sisters do not interact with the outside world except in matters of grave necessity. But as soon as Rita entered the convent her vocation was in jeopardy.

During her first month in the convent, Rita contracted pneumonia and had to be given permission to go to the hospital. Later Rita had to leave the convent again to have her tonsils removed. Her superiors began to wonder about her ill health. Rita threw herself into her new life accepting menial work assignments; laundry, baking, floor scrubbing; all with the knowledge that she was performing her work for Jesus.

In the first several months of her novitiate Rita's uncle, Nick, came to visit to inform her that Grandmother had died and that her Mother needed her. He tried to convince her to leave the cloister but Rita was resolute. She knew that God had called her to a life in the cloister.

Young Rita began to experience a constant swelling in her knees. The source of the affliction was unknown and gradually worsened. Rita's knees were swollen and constantly filled with fluid. She could walk but soon kneeling became almost impossible. A vote was scheduled for Sister Rita's full admittance to the novitiate but her poor health forced a postponement of the vote.

Mother Superior was very concerned about Rita's poor health. The monasteries were filled with postulants. In the 1940's most superiors believed that if a postulant did not have good health, it was God's way of showing that she did not have a vocation. Mother Superior granted Rita an extra six months trial period.

On Rita's twenty second birthday her mother, Mae visited her in the convent. They spent time together visiting through the grille that separates sisters from the public. Mae had come to realize that reconciliation with Rita was the best course of action. It was a joyful time for both of them. The relationship was renewed.

One of the older professed nuns encouraged Rita to find a way to kneel. Without the ability to kneel she would be sent home. So at great personal cost she forced herself to kneel, shifting her weight from shin to shin. Rita was determined to claim her place. Her determination paid off. In October of 1945 the community voted for full admittance. Rita received her new habit and veil one month later.

Bishop Schrembs was the presider at the investment ceremony. It was a sort of wedding day for Rita. After being dressed in a wedding gown she was then vested in the brown habit and white veil of the Franciscan order. The Mother Superior gave Rita's mother the honor of choosing her name. Mae chose "Angelica," because she said throughout life Rita was an angel to her. The solemn ceremony was attended by Rita's mother and many of her aunts and uncles.

Rita's new life had begun, a life dedicated to perpetual adoration of Jesus in the Blessed Sacrament. She was no longer to be known as Rita Rizzo but as Sr. Mary Angelica of the Annunciation.

Sr. Mary Angelica was now considered a novice and was one step closer to taking vows in the Franciscan Order. She and her mother began consistent communication in letters and visits (allowed every sixty days.) But her swollen knee problem still plagued her. She needed an answer.

Sancta Clara Monastery

In 1945, John O'Dea, a retired steel plant owner in Canton, Ohio and his wife Ida decided to donate their sprawling mansion to the Diocese of Cleveland. There was one stipulation: it was to be used specifically for perpetual adoration of the Blessed Sacrament. The O'Dea estate was a 24 room Tudor mansion situated on 15 acres of lush landscape, surrounded by a small forest.

The Bishop was delighted with the offer and discussed it with Mother Mary Agnes, Abbess of the Poor Clares of Perpetual Adoration. He asked her to establish a new community in Canton. She was grateful for the opportunity to advance the availability of Eucharistic Adoration. She called on six of her Sisters to pioneer a new foundation in Canton.

Mother Agnes chose two of her senior council members, Mother Clare and Mother Luka to oversee the renovations of the mansion and establish the new Franciscan community. Along with them Mother Agnes chose three junior sisters. Sr. Angelica was among them. It was highly unusual for a sister to be sent back to her home town but Mother Agnes felt this change was a final option for Sr. Angelica's health problems. Maybe her swollen knees would be helped by a dwelling with fewer steps. The decision was made. Sr. Angelica's knees would find relief in Canton and she would continue her journey toward final vows or she would be dismissed from the Order and asked to return to lay life.

On October 1, 1946 John O'Dea transported the six nuns to his mansion at 4200 North Market Street in Canton. It was a day of mixed emotions; joy at the thought of a new venture and sorrow at leaving Mother Agnes and the other nuns at the motherhouse in Cleveland. The next morning, October 2nd, Sister Angelica awoke in her new surroundings to find that her knees were completely normal. The swelling had disappeared. The religious community was astonished.

Mother Clare saw the healing of Sr. Angelica's knees as a sign from God. Preparations were quickly made for Sr. Angelica to make her first vows.

CHAPTER 12

Renovations

The luxurious O'Dea mansion needed much renovation to turn it into a monastery. The sisters needed a refectory, infirmary, dormitory, and most importantly a chapel. Work began immediately to transform the large dining room into a temporary chapel until a separate building could be constructed.

During this time of renovation Sister Angelica was in her canonical year; a period of prayer and study, a sort of immersion in the contemplative life. Sisters in this year were not allowed to have any contact with outside visitors, family or friends. But every day a lay person drove the group of Sisters to St. Peter Catholic Church, just 3 miles away to attend morning Mass with Msgr. George Habig, pastor and former spiritual advisor to young Rita Rizzo. Sr. Angelica's mother would attend morning Mass hoping to catch a glimpse of her daughter.

Finally on January 2, 1947 amidst a snow and ice storm Sr. Angelica professed first vows in the presence of Bishop McFadden, Mother Clare, her own mother, Mae Francis, Rhoda Wise, and the Poor Clare community.

As renovations moved forward the leadership skills of Sister Angelica began to emerge. She had great determination and a strong work ethic. Sr. Angelica was closely involved in the construction of the new chapel.

Gradually, more young women came to the monastery and the community grew. Sr. Angelica had a strong personality and the close living quarters of a monastery exaggerated conflicts and rivalries. Community living became a study in love, patience, and carrying the cross of Jesus. But the joy of her deepening relationship with Jesus overcame all obstacles.

The Poor Clare's charism is to adore the Lord in the Blessed Sacrament every hour of the day and night. Since the new Sancta Clara Monastery community was so small the Mother Superior enlisted the help of local lay people to fulfill the 24 hour Eucharist Adoration schedule. One volunteer adorer was Mae Francis.

Mae had grown in her love of Jesus and the Catholic Faith. She could only visit her daughter once every two months but she felt spiritually

connected to her every time she visited the Blessed Sacrament. It was a love they shared to-gether.

One afternoon Sr. Angelica was informed that she had a visitor in the parlor. Assuming it was her mother she opened the door and was shocked to find her Father, John Rizzo waiting to see her. After the initial shock Sr. Angelica felt only pity for the broken man she saw before her.

A bit of awkward small talk took place. Then her father apologized for all he did to hurt her and her mother. He asked permission to visit her again. She consented. When her mother found out she was furious. A sister is allowed one visitor every two months. Sr. Angelica voiced her con-cerns to the Mother Superior. Mother told Sr. Angelica she would write to her father and inform him that Mae had priority in visits. Six months lat-er John Rizzo died of a heart attack.

On Jan 2, 1953, after almost 10 years since she first set foot in the monastery Sister Angelica professed final vows in the new chapel of the Sancta Clara Monastery in front of her Mother Superior and her Franciscan community during a special Mass celebrated by Msgr. George Habig.

The Process of Becoming a Nun

Candidate or Postulant

Person lives in community with the sisters discerning her personal call to serve and live in community.

Novitiate

When a woman enters the novitiate, she is known as a novice and is called "Sister."

The **canonical novitiate** is a year especially dedicated to prayer, exploring the meaning of the vows and delving more deeply into religious life and the unique spirit or character of the community.

Temporary vows or First vows

The novice professes temporary vows, commonly called first vows, which are canonically binding for a particular length of time, often ranging from one to three years. During this time, the sisters engage in ministry and live in community. At the end of this period, the vows can be renewed.

Perpetual Vows

Perpetual vows commonly called final vows, are professed anytime three to nine years after temporary vows. The time may vary according to the tradition of the community. Perpetual vows are professed for life.

CHAPTER 13

The Injury

Sister Angelica was performing her duties one day in 1956 using a scrubbing machine to clean the floors in the monastery. The scrubbing machine kicked sideways and knocked Sister Angelica against the wall. She fell to the floor in terrible pain. "It was horrible," said Joan Frank, a former nun who witnessed the accident. "Angelica was in intense pain."[14]

The injury caused her great pain for weeks and the weeks turned into months. Gradually two years of limping misery passed. Doctors tried traction, shots in the spine, even a full body cast but nothing alleviated Sr. Angelica's pain. The decision was made for spinal fusion surgery. Sister Angelica was 33 years old.

The evening before surgery she lay in her hospital bed. The surgeon came to her room to inform her there was a fifty-fifty chance she would

never walk again. Sister Angelica was terrified. At that moment she made a solemn promise to God, "If you let me walk again, I will build you a monastery in the South."

Sister Angelica spent four months in the hospital after the operation. She was sent home with a back brace and crutches. Even though she walked with great difficulty Sr. Angelica was true to her promise. She spoke to the Mother Superior about her vow to build a monastery in the South, explaining her promise to God the night before her operation.

Many obstacles were in the path of young Sister Angelica to fulfill her dream of a monastery in the South. First, she needed the blessing of her Mother Superior and second, the Bishop of the Diocese needed to sign off on her request. Special permission was also needed from Rome for her to become a Mother Superior since she was so young.

But young Sr. Angelica was determined. She wanted to go South and establish a monastery that would be dedicated to the "Negro apostolate...It would be a monastery of Eucharistic adoration that would ceaselessly make reparation for all the insults and persecution the Negro race suffers and implore God's blessing and graces upon a people dear to the Heart of God."[15]

After months of delays, the local bishop finally gave a positive response to her request but with the stipulation that the new monastery be able to support itself. Sister Angelica had already been thinking about how to raise money for the new monastery. She had the idea of selling fishing lures to local anglers. With the blessing of her Mother Superior, Sister Angelica launched "St. Peter's Fishing Lures."

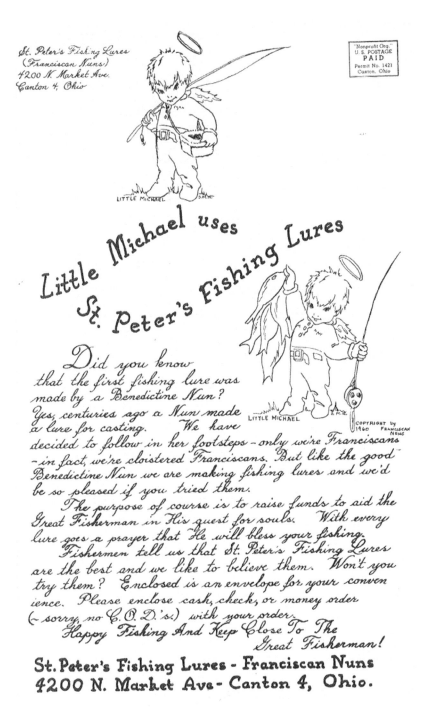

St. Peter's Fishing Lures
(Franciscan Nuns)
4200 N. Market Ave.
Canton 4, Ohio

"Nonprofit Org."
U. S. POSTAGE
PAID
Permit No. 1421
Canton, Ohio

LITTLE MICHAEL

Little Michael uses
St. Peter's Fishing Lures

LITTLE MICHAEL

COPYRIGHT by 1960 FRANCISCAN NUNS

Did you know that the first fishing lure was made by a Benedictine Nun? Yes, centuries ago a Nun made a lure for casting. We have decided to follow in her footsteps – only we're Franciscans – in fact, we're cloistered Franciscans. But like the good Benedictine Nun we are making fishing lures and we'd be so pleased if you tried them.

The purpose of course is to raise funds to aid the Great Fisherman in His quest for souls. With every lure goes a prayer that He will bless your fishing. Fishermen tell us that St. Peter's Fishing Lures are the best and we like to believe them. Won't you try them? Enclosed is an envelope for your convenience. Please enclose cash, check, or money order (– sorry, no C.O.D.'s) with your order.

Happy Fishing And Keep Close To The Great Fisherman!

St. Peter's Fishing Lures - Franciscan Nuns
4200 N. Market Ave - Canton 4, Ohio.

• 73 •

The initial response was disappointing. But soon a national Catholic publication found out about the fishing lures and published an article that gained national attention. After a slow start orders began pouring in. But there was one more bump in the road for Sr. Angelica.

Another Sister in the Sancta Clara community, with more seniority than Sr. Angelica had approached the Mother Superior for permission to start her own monastery. Angelica was furious but Mother Veronica found a simple solution. Each Sister was to write a letter to her prospective Bishop, mail it on the same day and wait for the response. The first Sister to receive a positive response would be given permission to move forward.

A week after both letters were sent Sr. Angelica received a letter of response from Archbishop Thomas Toolen of Mobile, Alabama. His two word answer to her request: "Ya'll come!"

CHAPTER 14

Our Lady of the Angels

In 1961, the nuns settled on a 15-acre plot in Irondale, Alabama, a suburb of Birmingham. The cost was $13,000; the exact amount raised by the fishing lure venture. They rented a small house and began building. Soon after the move to Alabama a woman from Canton expressed interest in joining the new community; her name was Mae Francis. Sister Angelica, now Mother Angelica, became the mother superior to her own mother.

Mae Francis made final vows in 1965. She was given the religious name Sister Mary David of the Infant Jesus. She served the community for 17 years until her death in 1982. She is buried in the monastery crypt directly below Mother Angelica; mother and daughter, together in life and in death.

As word spread among the locals about the building of a Catholic monastery in Birmingham donors came forward with great generosity.

Bricks, concrete, flooring, monetary donations all began to come in. A local grocery store owner promised the Sisters free food. Even the construction workers donated their time and talent without assurance of a paycheck.

Our Lady of the Angels Monastery in Irondale, Alabama was dedicated May 20, 1962. The Sisters supported themselves selling fishing lures but the business stalled. Roasted peanuts followed that. The "Li'l Ole Peanut Company" did so well that by 1968 the monastery debt was paid off. The peanut company was disbanded after a local supplier demanded a kickback.

Mother Angelica shows a model of her monastery to Archbishop Toolen.

In 1971 Mother Angelica had a deep charismatic experience of the Holy Spirit as a priest prayed over her. She was given the gift of tongues and a great love of the Word of God. The Scripture came alive for her. Bishop Vath of Birmingham, gave her permission to accept local speaking engagements. Her popularity as a faith-filled yet entertaining speaker grew.

Mother Angelica began writing short teachings about the Bible and the Catholic Faith in front of the Blessed Sacrament. The community decided to turn these teachings into mini books. A local radio station aired short segments that Mother Angelica recorded.

By 1976 Mother Angelica had written 50 mini books. The mini books became so popular that the Sisters bought a printing press and printed the books in house shipping them worldwide. She also recorded hundreds of teachings on audio cassette which were made available to the public.

Word spread about this charismatic cloistered nun from Birmingham and television networks began to request interviews. Mother Angelica realized she could reach an exponential number of souls through television, teaching them about the love of Jesus Christ. Again with her Bishop's permission she accepted invitations on local and national television networks.

In 1978 the community decided to have Mother Angelica record a four-part 30-minute television series named "The Hermitage" to be aired on broadcast outlets across the country. The Christian Broadcast Network loved it and requested that she record sixty more programs. The Sisters were delighted.

The series was being recorded at the studios of a local CBS affiliate in Birmingham. Mother Angelica became aware that the local affiliate planned to air a blasphemous movie called "The Word." She challenged the president of the studio not to air it. He dismissed her concern. She made an ultimatum that if he aired the program she would never come to his studio again. He scolded her because she needed his studio. But in true form just like her famous bargain with God she informed the studio executive that she would build her own studio.

After her encounter with the studio executive, Mother Angelica went back to her monastery in distress. Her sisters were very supportive. The monastery was in the midst of building a new garage. The decision was made to expand the garage building and make a television studio. The community had no money, no knowledge of television and no long-term plan. That day the seed of the Eternal Word Television Network was planted. The seed sprouted and the little sapling grew by grace, prayer, determination and hard work into what is now the largest Catholic media network in the world.

CHAPTER 15

History of Accomplishments

Mother Angelica was the first woman to apply for and receive an FCC license for satellite television.

EWTN received its license on January 27, 1981 becoming the first Catholic satellite television station in the United States.

June 26, 1981: Mother Angelica receives papers from the Vatican giving her permission to carry out her television work.

August 15, 1981: EWTN begins transmitting four hours of programs to 60,000 homes. The network is funded completely by viewer contribution. Cable operators are offered EWTN free of charge.

November 1982: Mother Angelica presents Pope John Paul II with a model of the EWTN satellite dish.

August 15, 1983: "Mother Angelica Live" debuts on EWTN. In two years EWTN has grown to 31 states on 95 cable systems.

1984: "Mother Angelica Live" is nominated for the Award for Cable Excellence by the cable industry. She wins the Gabriel Personal Achievement Award from Catholic broadcasters. She is presented with the Golden Blooper Award.

1985: EWTN is now on more than 220 cable systems covering almost 2 million homes.

1985: "60 Minutes" airs an interview with Mother Angelica.

1986: EWTN expands to 24 hour programming on a new satellite.

1987: Mother Angelica launches two active religious orders: Order of the Eternal Word for men, and Sister Servants of the Eternal Word for women.

September 1987: EWTN airs complete live coverage of Pope John Paul II's visit to the United State.

1989: Mother Angelica goes to Rome seeking the Pope's blessing for a shortwave radio network.

1992: With huge donations from Dutch millionaire Piet Derksen and New Orleans Real Estate Developer Joseph Canizaro, Mother Angelica launches WEWN, the largest privately owned international short wave radio network. The potential listening audience is 600 million souls.

1995: EWTN is now carried in 42 countries in Europe, Africa, Central and South America.

August 15, 1995: Mother Angelica reveals plans to move her community of Sisters to a self-sustaining farm with chapel 50 miles north of Birmingham in Hanceville, Alabama

1995: Time Magazine names Mother Angelica as the Most Influential Roman Catholic Woman in the United States.

1996: Mother Angelica receives a miraculous message from the Divine Child Jesus while in Bogota, Columbia. "Build Me a Temple, and I will help those who help you."

1996: EWTN is beamed to the Pacific Rim, reaching Australia, New Zealand, China, Japan and the Philippines

1997: EWTN offers radio programs free of charge to any AM/FM radio outlet.

January 28, 1998: Mother Angelica is miraculously healed of her back and leg ailments while praying with Paola Albertini, an Italian mystic. The next day Mother Angelica dances in the studio without braces on her live television program.

December 1999: The Shrine of the Most Blessed Sacrament of Our Lady of the Angels Monastery is consecrated during a live broadcast. Mother Angelica's community of Sisters will live here. Price tag: $35 million. The $35 million was donated by 5 donors.

2000: Mother Angelica has a near death experience which she shares with her audience, saying she now has no fear of death.

Early 2001: Mother Angelia has a stroke which paralyzes half of her face. She goes on the air with a drooping mouth and black eye patch.

December 24, 2001: Mother Angelica has a massive life-threatening stroke that is completely debilitating.

2003: Mother Angelica is inducted into the Cable TV Pioneer Class of 2003

2004: Alabama Broadcasters Association names Mother Angelica "Citizen of the Year."

2004: EWTN reaches 100 million homes in 110 countries

2009: Mother Angelica is awarded the "Pro Ecclessia et Pontifice" by Pope Benedict XVI: the highest honor a Pope can bestow.

2004 – 2016: EWTN grows exponentially as Mother Angelica is confined to her bed, suffering silently for the network and the world.

March 27, 2016: Mother Angelica goes to her eternal reward.

(History of Accomplishments provided by EWTN)

Discussion Questions

The Backdrop

Rita's parents had an explosive relationship. What was your parents' relationship? How did that affect your image of marriage?

Reflections:

"Love is patient, love is kind.."   1 Corinthians

The Backdrop

John abandoned his wife and daughter when Rita was four years old. Have you ever felt abandoned? Did others come to your aid? Did the sorrow help you grow closer to God or did you push God away?

Reflections:

"My God, my God, why have you abandoned me.." Psalm 22

Prohibition

Rita grew up in a neighborhood nicknamed "the jungle." In what kind of neighborhood did you grow up? Were you comfortable or afraid in your neighborhood as a child?

Reflections:

"When I am afraid, I put my trust in you." ~ Psalm 56:3

The Faith

Rita was baptized when she was six months old. Do you know the date of your baptism? Do you celebrate the day of your baptism?

Reflections:

"Therefore go and make disciples of all nations, baptizing them in the name of the Father and of the Son and of the Holy Spirit, and teaching them to obey everything I have commanded you."
Matthew 28:19

The Divorce

Mae and John Rizzo were divorced when Rita was just six years old. What do you think was the public opinion of divorce in 1929? Are you or is anyone in your family divorced?

Reflections:

During grammar school years Rita had to suffer bias and prejudice because of her family situation. Have you suffered bias or prejudice?

Reflections:

"How long, O Lord? Will you forget me forever?" Psalm 13:1

The Church

Rita's pastor was assassinated in broad daylight when she was very young. Have you known anyone who was a victim of a violent crime? How did it affect you?

Reflections:

"The LORD is near to the brokenhearted and saves the crushed in spirit." Psalm 34:18

Depression

Rita's Mother suffered from severe bouts of depression. Have you had times of deep depression? Have you helped someone who suffered from depression?

Reflections:

"Be strong and courageous. Do not fear or be in dread of them, for it is the LORD your God who goes with you. He will not leave you or forsake you." Deuteronomy 31:6

High School

Rita took up baton twirling in high school. What extra-curricular activities were you involved in during high school? Rita helped raise money for her family. Did you hold a job in high school?

Reflections:

"Behold, children are a heritage from the LORD, the fruit of the womb a reward. Like arrows in the hand of a warrior are the children of one's youth." Psalm 127:3-4

The Illness

Rita had a life-threatening illness. Her mother was extremely concerned. Have you ever had to watch your child suffer a serious illness? Have you been extremely sick and not sure if or when you would get well? Did the situation make you pray more?

Reflections:

"Come to me, all of you who are weary and carry heavy burdens, and I will give you rest." Mathew 11:28

Rhoda Wise

Rhoda was ridiculed for reporting that she had visions of Jesus. Have you experienced ridicule for your faith? Rhoda offered herself as a victim soul. Have you ever offered to suffer for someone else?

Reflections:

"Blessed are you when people insult you, persecute you and falsely say all kinds of evil against you because of me. Rejoice and be glad, because great is your reward in heaven, for in the same way they persecuted the prophets who were before you." Matthew 5: 11-12

The Healing

Jesus healed Rita when she was in deep distress. Have you prayed for your own healing or the healing of another? Were you surprised if Jesus did perform a healing? There are many types of healing: physical, emotional, spiritual, etc. Which healing do you think is most important?

Reflections:

"Heal me, O Lord, and I will be healed; save me and I will be saved, for you are the one I praise." Jeremiah 17:14

The Call

Jesus called Rita to a deeper relationship with Him by becoming a nun… but Rita hated nuns. Has God called you to do something that seems ridiculous? What was your response? If you responded 'yes,' has your 'yes' borne good fruit?

Reflections:

"And I heard the voice of the Lord saying, 'Whom shall I send, and who will go for us?' Then I said, 'Here am I! Send me'." Isaiah 6:8

The Trial Period

Sr. Angelica had a very difficult trial period in the convent. Have you had a period in your life when you wondered if God had abandoned you? What was the outcome?

Reflections:

"Fear not, for I am with you; be not dismayed, for I am your God; I will strengthen you, I will help you, I will uphold you with my right-eous right hand." Isaiah 41:10

Sancta Clara

John and Ida O'Dea made an amazingly generous donation to the Diocese of Cleveland. Have
you given or received a lavish donation?

Reflections:

*"Whoever sows sparingly will also reap sparingly, and whoever sows
bountifully will also reap bountifully."* 2 Cointhians 9:6

Renovations and Vows

Sister Angelica and the other nuns had to leave their Cleveland community to begin the new foundation in Canton. It was bittersweet. Have you made a big move? Was it by choice or necessity? Where did you find God in the midst of it?

Reflections:

"Trust in the LORD with all your heart, and do not lean on your own understanding. In all your ways acknowledge him, and he will make straight your paths." Proverbs 3: 5-6

The Choice

Sister Angelica had the difficult choice of choosing between visits with her father or mother. Have you had to make difficult choices with your own family members? What was the result?

Reflections:

"But the LORD said to Samuel, "Do not look on his appearance or on the height of his stature, because I have rejected him. For the LORD sees not as man sees: man looks on the outward appearance, but the LORD looks on the heart." 1 Samuel 16:7

The Injury

Sister Angelica was terrified with the prospect of never walking again. She made a bargain with God. Have you made a bargain with God to attempt to overcome a difficult situation? What was the result?

Reflection:

"Count it all joy, my brothers, when you meet trials of various kinds, for you know that the testing of your faith produces steadfastness."
James 1:2

Going South

Sister Angelica was determined to move forward with her plan. She needed permission from others. Have you been stymied in your plans by others with more authority? Have you stopped others because of your authority? What did God teach you through the situation?

Reflections:

"Obey them that have the rule over you and submit yourselves: for they watch for your souls, as they that must give account, that they may do it with joy, and not with grief: for that is unprofitable for you." Hebrews 13:17

New Beginnings

Sister Angelica and her Sisters began a new foundation in Alabama with joy. There was also fear of the unknown. Have you taken a big step with joy but great fear of the unknown? Were the results positive?

Reflections:

"Be strong and of a good courage, fear not, nor be afraid of them: for the LORD thy God, he it is that doth go with thee; he will not fail thee, nor forsake thee." Deuteronomy 31:6

History of Accomplishments

How would you like your history of accomplishments to read?

Reflections:

"One thing have I desired of the LORD, that will I seek after; that I may dwell in the house of the LORD all the days of my life, to behold the beauty of the LORD, and to enquire in his temple. "
Psalm 27:4

Footnotes:

1 Raymond Arroyo: Mother Angelica: The Remarkable Story of a Nun, Her Nerve, and a Network of Miracles, 2005 Bantam/ Doubleday, page 8

2. Letter from Fr. John Riccardi to Bishop Schrembs

3. Canton Repository March 10, 1929

4. EWTN Family Newsletter July 1991

5. EWTN Family Newsletter July 1991

6. https://www.telegraph.co.uk/obituaries/2016/03/29/ mother-angelica-television-nun---obituary/

7. Dan O'Neill ,Mother Angelica: Her Life Story, Crossroad Publishing Company 1986, page 32

8. Raymond Arroyo: Mother Angelica: The Remarkable Story of a Nun, Her Nerve, and a Network of Miracles, 2005 Bantam/ Doubleday, page 14

9. Author interview with Elsie Machuga, girlhood friend of Rita Rizzo

10. Raymond Arroyo: Mother Angelica: The Remarkable Story of a Nun, Her Nerve, and a Network of Miracles, 2005 Bantam/ Doubleday, page 33

11. Author interview with Joanne Simia, cousin of Rita Rizzo

12. Dan O'Neill ,Mother Angelica: Her Life Story, Crossroad Publishing Company 1986, page 32)

13. Dan O'Neill ,Mother Angelica: Her Life Story, Crossroad Publishing Company 1986, page 37)

14. Author interview with Joan Frank, former Poor Clare nun at Sancta Clara Monastery

15. Raymond Arroyo: Mother Angelica: The Remarkable Story of a Nun, Her Nerve, and a Network of Miracles, 2005 Bantam/ Doubleday, page 75

Image Credits:

Page 11: Baby Rita and Mae Rizzo by Peggy Dolensky

Page 16: Photo of Our Lady of Sorrows at St. Anthony Catholic Church in Canton, OH by Christopher Cugini

Page 25: B/W painting of Fr. Joseph Riccardi by Angie Lereria

Page 26: Rita Rizzo at St. Anthony Catholic School by Peggy Dolensky

Page 29: Young Rita Rizzo and Mae Rizzo by Peggy Dolensky

Page 32: Rita Rizzo first majorette at McKinley High School by Peggy Dolensky

Page 42: Rita Rizzo and Rhoda Wise by Peggy Dolensky

Page 46: Photo of Jesus Carrying the Cross; station of the cross from St. Anthony Catholic Church, Canton, OH by Christopher Cugini.

Page 49: Msgr. George. Habig by Peggy Dolensky

Page 51: St. Paul Shrine in Cleveland, OH by Peggy Dolensky

Page 57: Sancta Clara Monastery by Peggy Dolensky

Page 60: Vows by Peggy Dolensky

Page 63: Monstrance by Peggy Dolensky

Page 65: Smiling Sister Angelica by Peggy Dolensky

Page 70: Sister Angelica on crutches by Peggy Dolensky

Books for further reading:

Her Name Means Rose; by Karen Sigler, SFO, EWTN Publishing

Mother Angelica: The Remarking Story of a Nun Her Nerve and a Network of Miracles by Raymond Arroyo, 2005, Doubleday/Random House

My Life with Mother Angelica by Sister M. Raphael, PCPA; 2015 Our Lady of the Angels Monastery

Mother Angelica: Her Life Story, by Dan O'Neil, 1986, Crossroad Publishing

ABOUT THE AUTHOR

Barbara Gaskell is the foundress and director of the Mother Angelica Tour in Canton, Ohio.   In 1989 she began St. Raphael Bookstore in a 300 square foot office. Today St. Raphael Center is a 7500 square foot facility that houses a gift shop, chapel, studio for the Living Bread Radio Network, outdoor rosary garden and Lourdes grotto. Barbara's life is dedicated to spreading the Good News of Jesus Christ.

ABOUT THE ILLUSTRATOR

Peggy Dolensky is a wife and mother who loves to draw. Peggy has neither art degrees or credentials. She simply loves to draw and is deeply inspired by her faith to draw saintly things. If her drawings reflect even a small bit of God's beauty that inspires others, she has accomplished her goal. Peggy was born and raised in Akron, Ohio. She and her husband John, live in the Akron area where they are raising their 7 beautiful children. Find Peggy's shop at etsy.com/shop/SaintlyStationery

Printed in the USA
CPSIA information can be obtained
at www.ICGtesting.com
CBHW071211200724
11747CB00017B/425